Money Cometh Hidden Wisdom

MONEY COMETH
HIDDEN WISDOM

DR. LEROY THOMPSON SR.

EVER INCREASING WORD MINISTRIES

DARROW, LA

Unless otherwise indicated, all Scripture quotations are taken from the *King James Version* of the Bible.

Scripture quotations marked MSG are taken from *THE MESSAGE*, copyright © 1993, 2002, 2018 by Eugene H. Peterson. Used by permission of NavPress. All rights reserved. Represented by Tyndale House Publishers, Inc.

Money Cometh! Hidden Wisdom

ISBN-13: 978-1-931804-01-1

Copyright © 2023 by Dr. Leroy Thompson, Sr. Ever Increasing Word Ministries

P.O. Box 7

Darrow, Louisiana 70725

Published by Ever Increasing Word Ministries.

P.O. Box 7 Darrow, LA 70725

Contents

Preface

On October 7th, 1994, I was asked to preach for a pastor named Bill McRay at Victory Fellowship Ministries in Nashville, Tennessee. It was undoubtedly a couple of months before I received the *money cometh* revelation from God. Pastor McRay and his wife prophesied powerful words to me that night. His wife would speak in tongues, and he would then give the interpretation.

Mrs. McRay: *I feel like God would like us to minister to you. Sometimes, He shows me or gives me a word in English. I don't know what it would mean to you but I will speak it out. Actually, it was two words. The first one was ACCOMMODATION and then CONSOLIDATION.*

(Message in tongues by Mrs. McRay)

[Interpretation by Pastor Bill McRay:] *Many things are about to happen quickly. Coming to pass very quickly in your ministry and in your life. And, it's gonna take wisdom, much wisdom to sort it out and to cause it to flow the way I want it to flow. Because time is short, and it will not be many years that these things will be done, but it will quickly —quickly, it will be done in your ministry and in your life.*

So, listen unto my Spirit, follow my Spirit closely, for I will give you blessing, blessing, blessing, and the enemy would come in to try to tear it apart, to try to direct it another way. But, don't allow it to be directed another way but be directed by my Spirit. And I have caused these things that looked like they could never be, to come to pass, and you'll be able to do everything that I've called you to do saith the Lord.

(message in tongues by Mrs. McRay)

[Interpretation by Pastor Bill McRay:] *Now I've called you to a body of believers, but I've also called you to my larger body, to my larger body. But, there will not be conflicting calls. I will bring them together so that you will be able to accomplish, you will be able to consolidate things in such a way that you will be able to do both in harmony and great blessing saith the Lord.*

It's been nearly 30 years since that prophecy was spoken, and I can say that everything Pastor McRay said to me has all happened. In that same year, I received and witnessed the revelation of *money cometh* from God in my life, and only a few years later, I had not only preached its series but also published the book *Money Cometh! To the Body of Christ.* If you've been high on a roller coaster, think about the ride to the top. It's been that way ever since. When it started, I couldn't stop it. God brought me from one level to another.

I believe this same prophecy I received in '94 is now intended to be shared with *you!* Read it over and take it personally.

Right now, God has the same two words for you: accommodation and consolidation. Many things are about to happen quickly in your life, but it will take much wisdom to sort them out and make them flow the way God wants them to flow. Ask yourself: *Am I ready for this?* Because it won't be long before these things are done. It will be done quickly in your life.

Listen to the Spirit of God, and closely follow. He will give you blessings, upon blessings, upon blessings! The enemy may try to tear it apart or direct it another way but don't allow it to be directed another way. Allow God's Spirit to direct you. God will cause things that look impossible to come to pass, and you will be able to do everything that He has called you to do.

Yes, God will bring together *everything* He called you to do, so there will not be any conflict in calls. You will be able to accomplish it all, and you will be able to consolidate things in such a way that allows you to do it all in harmony and with great blessings.

With that being said, the only factor left is your transformation.

Be not conformed to this world: but be ye transformed by the renewing of your mind, that ye may prove what is that good,

and acceptable, and perfect, will of God.

Romans 12:2

Receiving the prophecy is only the beginning for you. The divine principles taught in this book require you to *also* be ready for transformation. So as you prepare to begin producing in the spirit, you must first ask yourself:

Am I transformable?

Am I transition-able?

Am I prepared to fully operate in Romans 12:2 as I navigate the hidden wisdom of money cometh?

If the answer is *yes*, you're ready for what God has prepared next.

Introduction

The revelation of *money cometh* is not ordinary; it's super-natural. My life is a testament to it. Once a poor, country boy, raised on a farm, who walked a gravel road to school every day... now a multi-millionaire? It doesn't make sense, naturally. And you should never expect it to. When I think of my story, I recall Zechariah 4:6—it's "not by might, nor by power, but by my spirit, saith the Lord of hosts." I can tell you from experience that God desires for you to simply trust His Spirit and not waste time trying to figure your prosperity out.

Look at Jesus. He had the revelation of *money cometh* before anyone else. In Matthew 17:27, He told Peter, "Go thou to the sea, and cast a hook, and take up the fish that first

1

cometh up; and when thou hast opened his mouth, thou shalt find a piece of money: that take, and give unto them for me and thee"—Jesus was explaining a *money cometh* demonstration.

Have you ever gone fishing? When you cleaned the fish, did you find money in its mouth—enough money to pay your taxes? I'm sure it's never happened. It's not the natural way of getting money for taxes. This proves that the *money cometh* revelation and the instructions that come with it will not make sense in the natural realm. In the same way, God is looking to do divine demonstrations for you.

I couldn't explain my life if I wanted to. Our church, Word of Life Christian Center, owns 600 acres of land in the small town of Darrow, Louisiana. If anyone wants to build something in this town, they have to come to God because this belongs to Him. That's the way God wanted it for all His people. Believe it! It's time that you see large amounts of money coming to you that way. It's time you see city-shaking money. And it's time to shut up those conversations about barely making it. You serve an almighty God!

The kind of money I'm talking about does not come by salary or working multiple jobs. It doesn't matter how well you work or how long you've been working. Divine prosperity only comes by sowing, giving, and tithing, which we'll talk more about throughout this book.

I dare you to turn your salary into seed and see what happens. One morning, you'll walk into the office and tell your boss, "Thank you for the job, but I'm done here." I know it's possible because I did it. I walked in with a suit on, which was completely out of the dress code for someone working in tanks at a chemical plant. But since my boss had on his necktie, I wore my necktie that day too.

"Mr. Potter, thank you for the job," I said. "I know I was supposed to give a notice, but the Lord told me to quit today."

Mr. Potter was confused. "What you gonna do?"

"Preach the gospel," I said. "The Lord is going to take care of me."

Mr. Potter felt sorry for me at the time, but before he died, the Lord moved him into my neighborhood to witness the results. On a regular basis, he had to pass by my estate on his way to his house. A former superintendent of a company moved into a "house" next to his ex-employee who now lives in an "estate". Do you catch the difference? He couldn't deny all the productions God had done in my life. That's an example of what some of your employers and neighbors will see when you begin to walk in the *money cometh* anointing fully. Quite naturally, people will not understand you. I'm sure my neighbors are nervous because they never know what I'll update or add to my estate next. They have no idea how I got to where I am, but they do know who I represent. They know I love God and live a righteous, upright life.

My story should not be as uncommon as it is in the Body of Christ. It's time for the Church as a whole to rise in their finances, in a massive way. God needs a remnant of His people with plenty of money and wealth, and the question at hand is, *will that remnant include you?*

GOD'S WISDOM OVER MAN'S WISDOM

For years, Christians have mundanely tried to receive the prosperity they read about in the Bible through science of the mind studies, physical work, and sometimes, two and three jobs. But they become weary and never receive the hidden wisdom that God has prepared for them. Many can attest to working hard year after year, but when it comes time to buy something that they want or need, they have no choice but to leave it there or go borrow the money for it. This should not be the case! That's why this book is so important for the Body of Christ. The revealed things concerning our prosperity belong to us. Deuteronomy 29:29 states: "The secret things belong unto the Lord our God: but those things which are revealed belong unto us and to our children for ever, that we may do all the words of this law." We must act as if we know this is the truth and that we can financially operate in God's wisdom rather than man's wisdom.

Take a look at First Corinthians 2. Apostle Paul writes to the Christians living in Corinth:

(1) I, brethren, when I came to you, came not with excellency of speech or of wisdom, declaring unto you the testimony of God. (2) For I determined not to know any thing among you, save Jesus Christ, and him crucified. (3) And I was with you in weakness, and in fear, and in much trembling. (4) And my speech and my preaching was not with enticing words of man's wisdom, but in demonstration of the Spirit and of power: (5)That your faith should not stand in the wisdom of men, but in the power of God.

As Paul told them then, I'm saying the same to you today. When it comes to your finances (and everything else), your faith must not stand in the wisdom of men but in the power of God.

Paul goes on to say to the church of Corinth: *(6) Howbeit we speak wisdom among them that are perfect: yet not the wisdom of this world, nor of the princes of this world, that come to nought.*

What does he mean by "we speak wisdom among them that are perfect"? Who is considered perfect? He's talking about mature Christians. They are the ones to whom God's wisdom can be revealed, not those who have yet to mature. It can be dangerous to reveal mysteries to them.

Paul continues: *(7) But we speak the wisdom of God in a mystery, even the hidden wisdom, which God ordained before the world unto our glory (8) which none of the princes of this world knew: for had they known it, they would not have crucified the Lord of glory.* In other words, Paul is saying the reason they crucified the Lord was because they had no idea who He was. They lacked this kind of wisdom—God's wisdom. It proves, even more so, that the wisdom of God is hidden and not accessible to everyone. There are mysteries—including mysteries of prosperity—that can only be taught to you by the Holy Spirit.

Paul went on to write: *(9) Eye hath not seen, nor ear heard, neither have entered into the heart of man, the things which God hath prepared for them that love him. (10) But God hath revealed them unto us by his Spirit: for the Spirit searcheth all*

things, yea, the deep things of God. The apostolic words of
Paul here are crucial. A spiritual transaction must take place
between, "Eye hath not seen" in verse 9, and "God hath
revealed them to us by His Spirit" in verse 10. Verse 9 is
about a Christian who is still living by man's wisdom; verse
10 is about what happens when that person matures, hears
from the Holy Spirit, and starts living by God's wisdom.
The entire second chapter of First Corinthians needs to be
studied, as it breaks down how God's wisdom transpires.

*It is given to you to know the mysteries of the kingdom of
heaven, but to them it is not given. For whosoever hath, to him
shall be given, and he shall have more abundance: but whosoever
hath not, from him shall be taken away even that he has,* says
Jesus in Matthew 13:11-12. What does He mean exactly?
For whosoever has what? He's saying whoever has the mystery! That person *shall have more abundance.* In other words,
certain things must be revealed to you by the Holy Spirit
but will be hidden from those who will misuse them.

The revelation of *money cometh* is a hidden wisdom that
can only be revealed to a mature person with ears to

hear; it won't be revealed to those who trample on it. It's revealed to those who respect it, prophetically. The prophetic prosperity realm of God is for those who are *real*, which sadly means the average Christian may never see, hear, or understand it. It doesn't come by principles that men have set—nor does it come by confessions or creative vision boards. It's reverential and supernatural. It is divine instruction from God.

Money cometh is a powerful unfoldment of prosperity by the Holy Ghost, and we'll take steps in this book to unlock its hidden wisdom in your life.

PART I

13 Hidden Wisdom Steps of Money Cometh

Money cometh is a revelation from God that gives believers a sign to attack poverty and attract prosperity. When you say and believe the words *money cometh*, all lack, debt, and insufficiency in your life is attacked and all the prosperity that will come into your life is attracted.

– *Apostle (Dr.) Leroy Thompson, Sr.*

1

Walk in Holy Prosperity

God's prosperity is holy, and understanding its holiness is the first step toward walking in the hidden wisdom of *money cometh.* For prosperity to be holy, it must be connected to God, which means He has His hands on *everything* that you hold.

That's the reality of my story. God has His hands on everything that I have because He gave it to me. I recall a day, many years ago, on an early morning walk through my neighborhood, I noticed a woman I knew in the distance walking my way—she was walking because she had no car. When I got closer to her, I gave her $100. But as soon as

I did, God said to me, "That's nice, but I want you to buy her a car." Without hesitation, I bought her that car. That's how you know my prosperity belongs to God—He can tell me what to do with it and trusts that I'll listen. It makes the money in my hands and bank *holy prosperity*.

For many, the stagnation in their prosperity comes from the fact that they are not ready for this type of holiness in their finances. Someone can have tons of scriptures under their belt and pray in the spirit for hours a day, but the question would still stand, are they ready for *holy* prosperity? Are they ready to sow $50K into someone if God tells them to? You must be ready to "remember God" in every decision, even when you have millions available to you.

Let's read Psalm 1:1-3, which shows us just how holy prosperity functions:

"(1) Blessed is the man that walketh not in the counsel of the ungodly, nor standeth in the way of sinners, nor sitteth in the seat of the scornful. (2) But his delight is in the law of the Lord; and in his law doth he **meditate day and night**. (3) And he shall be like a tree planted by the rivers of water,

that bringeth forth his fruit in his season; his leaf also shall
not wither; and **whatsoever he doeth shall prosper.**"

These scriptures are giving you the key to more than
enough. In Psalm 1:2, we see "meditate day and night",
meaning never let God off your mind. Live with Him in
the morning, noontime, and late in the evening. Get to a
point where you can't get Him off your mind even if you
try. As soon as I open my eyes in the morning, He's there
on my mind, and He's there when I lay myself to sleep at
night. He's always there so I don't have time to think about
money. My mind is full of Him, and the money just keeps
on coming.

It may seem like this book is about going after money,
but it's not. It's about allowing money to come after *you*.
Position yourself to become so holy, so consecrated, and
so dedicated to God that the money starts looking for you
— and God starts looking for ways to use large amounts
of money *through* you. A principle to never forget: When
prosperity is holy, it never stops coming to you.

In Psalm 1:3, we read, "And [you] shall be like a tree

planted by the rivers of water, that bringeth forth [your] fruit in [your] season; [your] leaf also shall not wither; and whatsoever [you] doeth shall prosper." In order to bring forth fruit in your season, something has to be sown, right? Fruit doesn't come without a seed, so the seed *has* to lead. God gives us the seed to conquer money, but the average Christian won't go here because they are still trying to do it themselves. Whether they realize it or not, *money cometh* does not happen without the seed. When the revelation was first revealed to me by the Spirit, the physical act of sowing came with it. Therefore, when you meditate on the Word of God day and night, you *must* know how to sow, too. It goes together! Will you buy a car and sow it into someone if God tells you to do it? You see, you can't leave out God's instructions about sowing. It's only *then* that "whatsoever [you] do shall prosper."

I'm not just reading scriptures when I read Psalm 1:1-3; I'm living them. I meditate on His Word all hours of the day and night, and everything I do prospers. Declare today that the same will happen to you.

REMEMBER THE LORD

Paycheck-to-paycheck living is a beast. I used to know that beast, but I'll never know him again. I kicked him out of my house a long time ago, and now it's your turn. The power lies within you to change your situation. If that's not the truth, why would God allow Deuteronomy 8:18 in the Bible? It reads: *But thou shalt remember the Lord thy God: for it is he that giveth thee power to get wealth, that he may establish his covenant which he sware unto thy fathers, as it is this day.*

You absolutely have the power to get wealth. But here's where many miss it—when you read Deuteronomy 8:18, there should be a pause at "thou shalt remember the Lord thy God". Don't be so quick to jump to "the power to get wealth". The major key here is keeping God contained in all your transactions. Your wealth from God is a covenant wealth, not something for you to boast about or do whatever you want to show off. God wants to use *you*, and when He can, He will bless you in the process. You must be ready to "remember the Lord" in every part of your life and finances. That's holy, clean prosperity backed by God.

***

When the Apostle Paul addressed the church of Ephesus, he spoke to them about grace and prayed two powerful prayers: one is in the first chapter of Ephesians and the other is in the third chapter. He explains the quality of love someone has to have for God and their fellow men and women in order to walk in divine prosperity. In Ephesians 3:20, he begins the prayer: *Now unto him that is able to do exceeding abundantly above all that we ask or think, according to the power that worketh in us—*. "The power that works in you" has to actually be at work or you won't be able to function in holy prosperity.

Let me break this down further. Those trusted with divine, holy prosperity never leave God out, in any circumstance. Their lives are too consecrated to act like a clown in the flesh. They don't show off without showing God. They're not high-minded, and they don't forget to walk in love with their fellow men and women. They also know how to cut people out of their lives who are not aligned with God's way of doing things. The power of God is at work in them. These people are rich *and* holy!

Money cometh is pure; therefore, truly loving God is a part of it. It's a training component that has to take place before God can trust you with the good of immeasurable wealth and prosperity. God has to be in your heart and soul.

Are you ready to bless your enemies if God tells you? Are you willing to forgive someone who said something against you? You have to decide to be clean in your heart and not travel in the trash traffic of the world's system. In other words, the hidden wisdom of *money cometh* doesn't roll with someone who would get rich and then dishonor their spouse, or get rich and try to manipulate others. You

DR. LEROY THOMPSON SR.

can't use manipulation and then expect God to bless you financially in *His* divine way. We're talking about holy people — those who will remember God, His instructions, and His holiness, regardless of how much money they have.

20

2

Connect to Heavenly Prosperity

God's prosperity for you is spiritual *first*. Only after you receive the revelation and learn how to function in the spirit with it will it manifest in your life physically. That's why there's something *you* will have to do with spiritual understanding, first, and in this case, prayer and scripture reading doesn't cut it. Prayer doesn't move money. Quoting scriptures doesn't cause money to manifest. The thing you must do with spiritual understanding is called "give".

"Take care of My house," God says in Malachi 3:10. "You're trying to get Me to take care of your house, but you should take care of My house first." And you'll see

21

when He says "prove me now" in that verse, He's saying, "If you can, put Me on the spot. I dare you to try me." Let's read it fully: "Bring ye all the tithes into the storehouse, that there may be meat in mine house, and prove me now herewith, saith the Lord of hosts, if I will not open you the windows of heaven, and pour you out a blessing, that there shall not be room enough to receive it" (Malachi 3:10).

Tithing and giving establish your proper connection with heavenly prosperity. As a result, if you aren't a tither and giver, you won't be able to connect with heavenly prosperity. When God tries to get something to you, He looks for you to open the right doors. For heavenly prosperity to flow, tithing and giving are the right doors to open.

Now, suppose you've been tithing for 25 years and you're still in debt. Well, then something is wrong! That's not God; that's you and whoever's preaching to you. If you're in a begging church, leave. You can't tithe and sow and stay broke. It's a divine principle. If you're in that type of situation and wondering when the "windows of heaven" will come open for you, I assure you that they can open right now if you reposition your mindset, actions, and connection and allow it to flow.

STEWARDING HEAVENLY PROSPERITY

Heavenly prosperity is only waiting on you to walk in unwavering stewardship with your giving, sowing, and tithing.

Think about a rubber band for a moment— it's not good for anything when it's just lying around. The rubber band's real glory is revealed when it is stretched. In the same way, there is tremendous power in our stewardship but only when it is stretched.

What is stewardship? Stewardship is discipleship plus obedience. When a disciple is obedient with money, he's walking in stewardship. And let me tell you the weight of regret and poverty are far greater than the weight of stewardship. The purpose of stewardship (with our tithe, seed, and giving) is to make our emotions uncomfortable and to cause those emotions to bow their knee to the King of Kings and Lord of Lords. In turn, it releases massive, heavenly prosperity.

To walk in stewardship, you must first know that your election to live in prosperity is of God. It's already settled. Apostle Paul says to the church of the Thessalonians, "We give thanks to God always for you all, making mention of you in our prayers; Remembering without ceasing your work of faith, and labour of love, and patience of hope in our Lord Jesus Christ, in the sight of God and our Father; Knowing, brethren beloved, your election of God" (1 Thessalonians 1:2-4).

This election is not about you voting for God; it's about God voting for *you*. Before you were born, He voted and decided that you would prosper. But it won't happen without diligence. Second Peter 1:10 states, "Brethren, give diligence to make your calling and election sure: for if ye do these things, ye shall never fall." Therefore, give diligence to make your financial calling and financial election sure! If you do so, you'll never fall financially again.

We know "many are called, but few are chosen" (Matthew 22:14). Well, it's the diligence and proper response that separates those who are chosen from those who are not. In Romans 11:5, we read, "Even so then at this present time also there is a remnant according to the election of grace." There is a financial remnant who are chosen because they simply respond to the call, according to the prosperity election of grace. Until you are a part of that chosen remnant, by choosing your financial call through diligence, your heavenly prosperity will be frozen.

THE *STARTING 5* OF STEWARDSHIP

The "starting five" of a basketball game is a group of five players that a coach sends to the court to begin a game. The starting five of stewardship are tithe, offering, special seed, vows/pledges, and alms. Giving within any of those creates a prosperity rhythm. Doing it means taking action in the natural realm toward what you really believe is going on in the spirit realm and bringing those two worlds together.

Tithes and offerings are reminders that it's not you—not your looks, mind, intelligence, or abilities—that creates or connects you to divine prosperity. You're reminded that you can't do it on your own. You are taking the attention off yourself and off what you see going on around you. It makes sure that God gets the credit, no matter what. It brings the vision and shifts your financial status and your financial capacity for more.

Further studying of the starting five of stewardship:

- **Tithe:** Gen. 14:18-34, 15:1
- **Offering:** Psalm 96:1-8
- **Special/Project Seed:** Luke 7:1-5
- **Vows/Pledge:** Psalm 50:15

- **Alms:** Matthew 6:1-4

***

So, how do you go from realizing prosperity on the inside of you to having prosperity on the outside yourself? Stewardship. It's what God gave us to connect us to His covenant, and His covenant is not a mutual fund; it's a miracle fund. Having stewardship in your giving, sowing, and tithing is what accesses and releases what's in God's covenant for you. When your stewardship is able to reach out and touch what God has provided for you, no one can stop it.

The *money cometh* revelation has no problem bringing the money to you when you've taken hold of it with stewardship. Giving is the thing that puts you in the flow to receive. If your hand is always out, *money cometh* won't work. There has to be a balance. Why? Because when the *money cometh* anointing comes on your life, it'll take you places you never thought you could go.

There is a time to pray and there is a time to do. Stewardship is our *way of doing.* It's saying, "I believe what God is saying; I believe what God's doing; I believe what God promised, and my actions are backing up what I am saying. It's releasing God's heavenly covenant in my life."

3

Put the Holy Spirit in Charge of Your Finances

Godly prosperity has to be led by the Holy Ghost. That means He leads you in what you're buying and where you're going, at all times. It's important that you're led, because if not, with so much money coming, you could become unhinged on your own. Before putting you in that position, the Holy Spirit wants to know, "Are you going to put me in charge of this prosperity that you're speaking about? Can I tell you *no?*"

Many hesitate with the thought of giving God charge of their money because they think God is a tightwad. He's

29

not. Let's say you see two things that you want: one is $35K and the other is $85K. Trust me, He wants you to get the best one! That's His nature. That's how real it is. Once you learn the principles, it's very easy to be rich, because riches are waiting on *you*.

In Romans 8:14, we learn, "For as many as are led by the Spirit of God, they are the sons of God." Well, sons and daughters of God, you will have to be led in everything, including prosperity. You must be led *to* prosperity, and when you get *in* prosperity, the Holy Spirit will still be there to lead you.

Say this aloud, "Holy Spirit, I put you in charge of all my finances right here, right now in Jesus' name!" There's nothing manipulative about saying it with power and force. It's moving you into a realm where your faith can catch hold of it—a place where you're doing things you don't understand but the Spirit is in charge.

I don't care how much you have in your bank or safe. Don't even worry about your little savings. Maybe you've been saving for retirement and saying, "I'm not going to touch that. I don't care what he says about sowing; I don't care how much he preaches to me; I'm not going to touch that!" And now, your prosperity is in that retirement! If God tells you to sow a seed out of that retirement, He's trying to get something to you so that you'll never have to worry about retirement again. You'll be in the "heyday" of your life pinching with that little retirement. You'll be living on survival when you could be living supernaturally. You should never swap your supernaturalness for survival! Give God charge of every penny you have. Say it aloud, continuously: "God, you can have it!"

It doesn't matter if you have a small nest of $20K or don't have any more than $3—give it to Him. In other words, let Him take charge of it and tell you what to do with it. Whatever you have will never make God nervous. He doesn't have to go into a prayer meeting to tell you what to do with it.

My hope is to help you see that at the end of the day, it's not about the "nest" you have tucked away. This is about a remnant of people that God wants to use in prosperity in a major way. And if God is going to use somebody, why not you? Say this aloud: "Lord, why not me? I yield! Use me financially!"

Get Rid of The Holes in Your Bag

4

Get Rid of The Holes in Your Bag

Ye have sown much, and bring in little; ye eat, but ye have not
enough; ye drink, but ye are not filled with drink; ye clothe
you, but there is none warm; and he that earneth wages earneth
wages to put it into a bag with holes.

Haggai 1:6

The book of Haggai is set in the context of a group of
Israelites who have misplaced their priorities. They became
more concerned with rebuilding their own, fancy houses,
while the temple (God's house) lay in ruins after being

33

destroyed years before. The prophet Haggai asks the Israelites in Haggai 1:4 (MSG), "How is it that it's the 'right time' for you to live in your fine new homes while the Home, God's Temple, is in ruins?" He goes on to reveal that this is the reason they've been struck with famine and drought. "Ye have sown much, and bring in little; ye eat, but ye have not enough; ye drink, but ye are not filled with drink; ye clothe you, but there is none warm; and he that earneth wages earneth wages to put it into a bag with holes (Haggai 1:6, KJV)." This means they couldn't make any real progress because they left God's house undone to focus on their own. It caused holes in their bags.

Here's the thing you must understand for your own life: If you are more worried about your house than the house of the Lord, you will always have holes in your bag, and listen, you obviously can't get a bag full when there are holes in it. So, if you wonder why your bag is not coming up full, it's because it has holes in it. You have to pinpoint how the holes got there in order to shut them closed.

For a minute you may think, "Oh, I don't have any holes in

my bag. I'm doing well." Well, check your life out again. Can you quit your job tomorrow and be taken care of with no limits for the rest of your life? Can you buy the estate you look at all the time, right now? Let's deal with your reality. How is your cup going to run over when there are any holes in it at all? You must first identify it so you can get it filled.

I've already done these things—closed the holes, and put the holy spirit in charge of my finances—and it works! May the same work for you, through the revelation, manifestation, and true demonstration of *money cometh.*

DR. LEROY THOMPSON SR.

5

See The Prosperity Presentation Before You

God promises and foretells your prosperity before it happens, laying out a presentation before you. The foretold presentation is actually a visitation that allows you to step off into an application so that a manifestation can take place. Prosperity does not come to you physically first. It comes to your mindset, your imagination, your will, and your consciousness. In other words, it's first made alive in your soul by the Holy Spirit.

The Bible says, "I wish above all things that you may prosper and be in health, even as your soul prospers" (3 John

1:2). Your soul has to prosper in order for your physical life to prosper. That's where it all starts. God will lay out a presentation—an internal presentation—before you, first.

In Genesis, we see how God laid a presentation out before Joseph, foretelling his prosperity in a dream. He gave Joseph a preview and didn't care about the pit, the people, Potiphar, or the prison up ahead. None of that could stop what God had in store for Joseph. And in the same way, when God shows you what He has in store, there's no outside force that can stop it.

Even before Joseph had the dream, his brothers already hated him. The dream just made them hate him more. Genesis 37:5 says, "Joseph dreamed a dream, and he told it to his brethren: and they hated him yet the more." As we keep reading through verse 11, we see that even his father rebuked him when he heard the dream.

(6) And [Joseph] said unto them, Hear, I pray you, this dream which I have dreamed: (7) For, behold, we were binding sheaves in the field, and, lo, my sheaf arose, and also stood upright; and, behold, your sheaves stood round about, and made obeisance to

my sheaf. (8) And his brethren said to him, Shalt thou indeed reign over us? or shalt thou indeed have dominion over us? And they hated him yet the more for his dreams, and for his words.

(9) And he dreamed yet another dream, and told it to his brethren, and said, Behold, I have dreamed a dream more; and, behold, the sun and the moon and the eleven stars made obeisance to me. (10) And he told it to his father, and to his brethren: and his father rebuked him, and said unto him, What is this dream that thou hast dreamed? Shall I and thy mother and thy brethren indeed come to bow down ourselves to thee to the earth? (11) And his brethren envied him; but his father observed the saying (Genesis 37:6-11).

What can we learn from this? When you're on the journey to prosperity—and God has shown you that you'll reign and have dominion in your finances—people who don't understand will want to rebuke you. They'll want to call you unspiritual but don't let them. The people who are broke, barely making it, and won't adhere to the message of prosperity from God, are the ones who are, in fact, unspiritual. The truth is that you simply know what's rightfully yours.

Now here's the thing: you're going to have to be ready to take the envy and rebuke. No one can do it for you. Leaving normal church folks behind and walking in prosperity will cause them to come against you, just as Joseph's family came against him. It's sad to say but that's how the current state of the Church thinks. And the world, outside of the Church, doesn't want God's people to rise in finances, because they know that prosperous, wealthy Christians will make sure God is in charge of everything their hands touch.

I'm here to tell you never to allow envy and rebuke to bother or hold you back from what's in store. Keep your eye on the presentation that God sets before you, both internally and in His word. Being prosperous is a promise from God that He will see through, no matter the circumstance if you let Him.

I've gone through pits and pit bulls, too, but none of that could hold me from God's presentation. I kept moving, and I continued to move because God is on my side. He showed me visions and shared prophecies with me before it all happened. His glory blinded the people who tried to stop it, and by the time they saw me again, they didn't know how I got out of where I used to be. I see the same happening to you. No one's lack of understanding can stop the perpetual blessings that belong to you.

GOD'S BRAGGING RIGHTS

If you're reading the Bible correctly, you'll notice that over and over God talks about prosperity, wealth, abundance, and increase. He talks about being the lender and not the borrower, being the head and not the tail. He brags about characters like Job, Abraham, and Solomon.

How do you feel when you read about how rich they were in the Bible? Do you have a religious cringe? You shouldn't. You should feel free. It pleases God to prosper you. So let Him do it. From this day forward, think pros-

41

perity, imagine prosperity, dream prosperity, walk prosperity, and talk prosperity based on what God has presented to you in His Word and in your life. It *has* to come because prosperity magnifies the Lord.

If God needed a bragging position, your prosperity would give it to Him. For instance, God had bragging rights with Job because Job had fully submitted to Him and was wealthy.

Job 1:1-3 reads, "There was a man in the land of Uz, whose name was Job; and that man was perfect and upright, and one that feared God, and eschewed evil. (2) And there were born unto him seven sons and three daughters. (3) His substance also was seven thousand sheep, and three thousand camels, and five hundred yoke of oxen, and five hundred she asses, and a very great household; so that this man was the greatest of all the men of the east."

Have you ever wondered why God revealed this to us about Job? It must be important to Him. After we learn about his spiritual uprightness in verse 1, we see in verse 3 that he also had substance. This makes it clear that spiritual uprightness and substance are meant to travel together. If you're in the spirit, substance belongs to you and is also looking for you.

The question is, would you let God have bragging rights with *you*? If you're walking in his ways, then you should have something to show for it! If you position yourself correctly, the money blessings will keep coming and flowing effortlessly. I speak from experience.

DR. LEROY THOMPSON SR.

6

Know Prosperity in Every Circumstance

In the previous chapter, we discussed Joseph's dream and the presentation God laid out before him. If we continue with that story, we can see what happened after his brothers betrayed him, threw him into a pit, and then sold him into slavery. Potiphar, the captain of Pharaoh's guard, purchased him. In the 39th chapter of Genesis, Joseph appears to be at his lowest point, in slavery, but an anointing remains on him, which eventually leads to him becoming master of Egypt.

(1) Joseph was brought down to Egypt; and Potiphar, an officer

45

of Pharaoh, captain of the guard, an Egyptian, bought him of the hands of the Ishmeelites, which had brought him down thither. (2) the Lord was with Joseph, and he was a prosperous man; and he was in the house of his master the Egyptian.

Genesis 39:1-2

If you want to walk in prosperity, you have to understand a statement we see in Genesis 39:2—"The Lord was with Joseph." That's the greatest statement of prosperity you'll ever hear. Notice the second part of that verse says, "And he was a prosperous man." In other words, make sure the Lord is with you, and prosperity is yours. Even in slavery, Joseph was a prosperous man. Let me tell you, when the prosperity anointing gets on you, it doesn't matter where you are, it *still* works.

Let's read further into the story: "And his master saw that the Lord was with him, and that the Lord made all that he did to prosper in his hand" (Genesis 39:3). Can we agree that the Lord has not stopped doing this? The Lord still has enough power to make everything prosper in your hands.

Joseph went on to find favor in the eyes of his owner, Potiphar, and was appointed overseer of Potiphar's household. All of Potiphar's possessions were then placed in the hands and trust of Joseph. During that time, the Lord blessed the Egyptians' house for Joseph's sake, and the blessing extended to everything he owned in the house and field. It is important to note that Joseph was prosperous even while enslaved. Even when his brothers conspired against him to put him in the worst possible situation, God's anointing on his life could not be stopped. As a result, we learn that regardless of our surroundings or circumstances, the prosperity anointing is always available to us.

PROSPERITY, EVEN IN A FAMINE

There's a famine in the Body of Christ that God wants to

DR. LEROY THOMPSON SR.

change. In Genesis 26, in the middle of a famine, God talks to Isaac about giving him countries and blessing him:

(1) And there was a famine in the land, beside the first famine that was in the days of Abraham. And Isaac went unto Abimelech king of the Philistines unto Gerar. (2) And the Lord appeared unto him, and said, Go not down into Egypt; dwell in the land which I shall tell thee of: (3) Sojourn in this land, and I will be with thee, and will bless thee; for unto thee, and unto thy seed, I will give all these countries, and I will perform the oath which I sware unto Abraham thy father. (4) And I will make thy seed to multiply as the stars of heaven, and will give unto thy seed all these countries; and in thy seed shall all the nations of the earth be blessed (Genesis 26:1-4).

So, why is God saying this to Isaac in the middle of a famine? Well, first, it's because of what Abraham, his father, had done before him. The next verse, Genesis 26:5, says, "Because Abraham obeyed my voice, and kept my charge, my commandments, my statutes, and my laws." Abraham obeyed God's voice and kept His commandments. But that's not it. Secondly, Isaac had to also do something. A few verses down, in verse 12, we see, "Then Isaac sowed in that land, and received in the same year a hundredfold: and the Lord blessed him."

What do we learn from this? We learn that the seed assassinates famine. The state of your condition doesn't matter to God; He doesn't pay any attention to it when you know how to sow. Isaac sowed in that land and received a hundredfold because God has no such thing as famine. Despite the conditions, the Lord decided to take it even further. The scripture adds, "and the Lord blessed him." So he had a hundredfold *and* was blessed by the Lord.

This proves that even in a famine God can get anything to you, at any time, from anywhere, through anybody. Isaac knew that, and you must, too. You can't afford to forget it. You must think, talk, pray, praise, worship, and meditate on the Word of God full of *that* type of confidence in Him.

Let's continue reading: "(13) And [Isaac] waxed great, and went forward, and grew until he became very great: (14) For he had possession of flocks, and possession of herds, and great store of servants: and the Philistines envied him."

Notice the word "possession" in verse 14. The sad truth is that the Church has been confessing long enough when it's actually time for possession. Most are living a famine life compared to the life that God wants them to live. As he did it for Isaac, he wants to do it for you. Those who grow and mature in prosperity know that no matter the situation they can always look to the Father to provide.

7

Get Out of God's Way

In Psalm 23:5, David writes, "Thou preparest a table before me in the presence of mine enemies: thou anointest my head with oil; my cup runneth over."

Let's answer the main question here, "Who is preparing the table?"

God.

You are not preparing the table for yourself. The scripture says He prepares it "before" you, which means before you get to the table, He's done it already. It means this is not about giving your input on what's on this table for you.

God puts on the table exactly what He wants to put on the table. He has heard all of your enemies' conversations and He knows your seed in the ground. Therefore, your seed and your enemies are the only two other things that help determine what's on your table. (You should be glad you have some enemies because your enemies are helping you get blessed. All the negative things they say about you only increase your blessings. The more they say or do against you, the more God blesses you. He will bless you just to shut their mouths.)

In Mark 4:26-27, Jesus says, "So is the kingdom of God, as if a man should cast seed into the ground; and should sleep, and rise night and day, and the seed should spring and grow up, he knoweth not how." Catch the phrase *he knoweth not how*. You see, everything God has planned and prepared is not for you to understand, overthink, or figure out. Let God do it as He sees fit. Do you understand what *money cometh* really means? It means when God gets ready to do something, money comes! Money needs an assignment, so He sends it out!

When God gets ready to bless you, He has the resources to get it done. So when He gets ready to do it, He needs you to get out of the way. When you need your figured-out plan in place to move forward, you're out of line. God doesn't operate like that. Trying to uncover the how and why messes up the entire flow. When operating within the apostolic and prophetic prosperity anointing, you are going to have to make a shift in your mind. Everything is not as straightforward as "two plus two equals four". You'll have to be in a flow with God to move as He wants you to move. And trust me, sometimes, when you don't understand what's going on, it's the best thing for you.

Luke 6:38 reads, "Give, and it shall be given unto you; good measure, pressed down, and shaken together, and running over, shall men give into your bosom. For with the same measure that ye mete withal it shall be measured to you again."

This scripture is loaded with the benefits of God. As it starts with "give," we see that's the only thing in this verse that God wants us to do. The rest of the scripture is about Him and what "shall be given unto you". Too often, we get involved on the wrong side of this verse.

We must understand that when God speaks forth, it will not change. When He said, "it shall be given", that's a word that will not return to Him void (Isaiah 8:22). He didn't say "might" or "in ten years"— He said it *shall* be given. That's it. "Give", and He *has* to do the rest. Now, have you ever wondered what God's "good measure, pressed down, and shaken together" will look like? How about what His "running over" looks like? A child of God should never be barely getting by with just enough, because that's not how our Father designed it to flow.

The Lord gets pleasure in blessing His children who are righteous, living right, and doing all that they can do for His glory. The second half of Psalm 35:27 says, "Let the Lord be magnified, which hath pleasure in the prosperity of his servant." When we get over on the wrong side of Luke 6:38, we strip God of His good pleasure to prosper us.

You have to get out of God's way enough to allow that

to happen. "Give" and get out of the way! Too often we don't receive the harvest because we are too busy trying to figure it all out. But you can't figure out your harvest. I wonder how many times God has tried to give you something and you turned it down because you couldn't figure it out; or, you didn't like the bill and didn't expect God to take care of it. I'm not talking about being reckless. I'm talking about when it's God's idea for you to have something—when it's God doing His "given unto you" part of the scripture. The harvest shows up but we are too analytical; we get too involved.

Remember, He prepares the table *then* He comes to get you. You have to submit to what's set when you arrive. When you are out of obedience with your harvest, the attraction of *money cometh* can't come to you as it should. You are supposed to have a free flow of money always flowing in your direction, but that only happens when you're open to God and not all wrapped up in your intellect, and when you're not talking about what you don't want, don't need, or can't get. Most times, your harvest is so vast that it's greater than what you can calculate, anyway.

When He says give, and the rest will be given, He's saying let Me have my pleasure, let Me shut your critics' mouths, let Me show them that my Word is true. That's what's at stake. With so many people in the world doubting God, there's *a lot* at stake if you don't allow God to prosper and position you. When you get out of God's ways and manifest (seated at the table God has prepared), it ends the conversations of your enemies and gives glory and pleasure to God.

8

Remember God Owns Everything

The first lesson of *money cometh* is: "God owns everything. I own nothing." The enemy's trick is to get you to believe that you own anything at all. But it *all* belongs to Him.

Sit with that truth for a minute.

The serpent entered the Garden of Eden and convinced Adam and Eve to believe they were lacking something. As if God hadn't already provided them with everything they'd ever need and more, they ate from the Tree of Knowledge of Good and Evil to gain some level of ownership. What happened to Adam and Even in the Garden of Eden was a complete flip—like a magnet flipped in the wrong direction. Since then, we've been trying to gain things that are already trying to reach us, and we believe we must own something here in order to make something happen.

The Word of God says, "The earth is the Lord's, and the fulness thereof; the world, and they that dwell therein" (Psalm 24:1). Is there anything else left for you to own? No, there isn't. God owns the world *and* you, too. This means you'll have to also give up ownership of yourself.

Trying to take ownership of ourselves is what causes the majority of people to never grow in the things of God and to hold on to their seed so tightly. In turn, this is where vanity, pride, and ego come in. If vanity wasn't there, you'd be overflowing with riches, but vanity causes you to do things for *yourself*, and forget that "God owns every-thing. We own nothing."

The truth is that everything you do is a response to what has already been done.

If everything you do is a response to what's already been done, then you must know what's been done, first. *Then,* you can respond accordingly. For instance, many believers give, but they don't give as they should. Why? Because they have yet to understand what's been given. When we don't have a revelation of what's been done, we don't respond to it properly.

Jesus says, "For God so loved the world, that he *gave* his only begotten Son—" in John 3:16. Paul states, "I live by the faith of the Son of God who loved me and *gave* himself—" in Galatians 2:20. None of this began with you. Before you existed, He gave it all. Therefore, we're highly mistaken if we sow money without first sowing ourselves. Say it aloud, "God owns everything. I own nothing." Understand that in your soul and commit to it; don't just visit it—commit to it and live there.

TAKE *SELF* OUT OF THE EQUATION

There's been something massively missing in the Body of Christ—and it's so simple to fix. It's a matter of getting over yourself. "If any man will come after me, let him deny himself—" Jesus said matter-of-factly in Matthew 16:24. In other words, take your*self* out of the equation, and let God's self in. The *self* you must lose is the one they told you was from this world, the one that has worry and fear running the show, the one that thinks there's not enough, the one holding on to the pain and traumas, building up walls to protect itself. That's the one you must take out of the equation. Many have missed this because their visions and desires still carry a little bit of leaven in them (Matthew 16:6; Galatians 5:9)—meaning their desires are clogged by their personal agendas and ideas of ownership.

Repeat it again, "God owns everything. I own nothing!" You're not from here, and you didn't choose this trip to Earth. You were sent here, and it's a common understanding that if someone sends you on a trip for them, that person is responsible for paying for the trip. It's the same with God. He sent you on this trip, and He is the One who will pay for it and supply your needs. Simply put: God sends, God pays.

When does the problem come in? When you forget you're on a trip and begin taking ownership of what you have here, putting up stakes. In Matthew 16:19-20, we read, "Lay not up for yourselves treasures upon earth, where moth and rust doth corrupt, and where thieves break through and steal: But lay up for yourselves treasures in heaven, where neither moth nor rust doth corrupt, and where thieves do not break through nor steal."

The Spirit of God, the wealth of God, and the *money cometh* anointing of God are all on the inside of you screaming, "Let me be! Remember where you come from. Remember who you are!" The idea of ownership has you prideful and functioning with an ego. Let it go. God owns everything; we own nothing. We are merely portals of His rich greatness.

The richest man to ever walk the Earth is Jesus, the Son of God. What could be more blessed than breaking bread and making more in your hands; turning water into wine when you need it; or collecting tax money from the mouth of a fish? It's evident—"God owns everything. We own nothing!" The Earth belongs to the Lord, but we have forgotten this wisdom—and forgetting it has held us back from operating as Christ did here. Overall, financial inversion is like a river behind a dam. It just sits there waiting for no one else but us to open it. For it to flow, there must be a *soul* inversion within us concerning this.

Our ownership lies in our heirship, but we cannot participate in the inheritance until we realize we are a son or daughter of God. To do that, we must deny ourselves (Matthew 16:24), and as mentioned earlier, take our *selves* out of the equation.

9

Realize You Are the Seed

Erroneous teaching produces erroneous thinking. It's improper to think we have to achieve or reach some goal to receive prosperity, when God said, "It's already done."

When Jesus therefore had received the vinegar, he said, It is finished: and he bowed his head, and gave up the ghost.

John 19:30

To fully understand the truth of "it's already done", you're going to have to switch from the law to grace. In the law, you're trying to earn it, but with grace, you simply *be* it.

You may think your seed is going to make you rich, or your tithe will make you rich, or even your offering will be the thing to make it happen. But God is saying, "Actually, *you* are the seed first, *you* are the tithe, and *you* are the offering." God designed the seed to show us how to function in this earth's realm as a god. Therefore, you're not *trying* to get prosperity, you *are* prosperity. The greatest seed that can be sown is yourself.

Jesus tells us in John 12:24, "Verily, verily, I say unto you, except a corn of wheat fall into the ground and die, it abideth alone: but if it *die*, it bringeth forth much fruit." Do you see yourself in that verse? When a seed is buried, it dies, and it's because of that death that it brings forth much fruit. In other words, the life of a seed cannot be released if it doesn't die.

This is why prosperity is not manifesting in the lives of many Christians—they don't know they are a seed and they aren't dead to their own agendas yet. The holy, God kind of prosperity belongs to crucified children of God; it belongs to people who have been persecuted because of righteousness, who don't care what others think of them, and who have died to themselves.

If you're going to understand the supernatural concerning this, you must first understand the natural. So if you can understand how a seed works in the natural world, you can see who you are and how to function in the supernatural realm.

God's purpose was always to plant someone in the earth's realm after His kind. Therefore, if you are God's seed and His seed is within you, then the problem with manifesting isn't with you—the problem is with your unrenewed, untransformed mind. You see, a spiritual birth and a sonship mentality are necessary to manifest godly prosperity.

It is long overdue for the children of God to leave their natural lineage behind and return to their spiritual lineage. God desires for His sons and daughters in the earth's realm to lose, or die to, *their* identity and instead walk in their divine identity in Him.

★★★

In John 10:17-18, Jesus says, "Therefore doth my Father love me, because I lay down my life, that I might take it again. No man taketh it from me, but I lay it down of myself. I have power to lay it down, and I have power to take it again. This commandment have I received of my Father."

Jesus is the Word of Life, and the Word of Life is a seed. If a man had taken Jesus' life, His life wouldn't have been a seed. But because He laid His life down—gave it up freely—it was sown. In the same way, you are not to be taken, you ought to be sown. You must give it up and lay down your life as and with a seed.

A seed only reproduces after its own kind. So as long as a seed is in your hand it abides alone. But if you want it to reproduce after its kind, you have to put it in the ground. Once you sow it, the seed will take over and tell the earth what to bring forth. The word and revelation *money cometh* is a seed. And when it has been sown into the earth, it tells the earth to bring forth *Money Cometh People*.

Before you sow a natural seed, you must first have a spiritual seed within you. You should have the Word of God undergirding you, giving you the courage and faith to obey God. You've got to die, lay your life down, to sow.

Now when you have the fruit of that seed harvested in your life, don't get so focused on what's there to eat. At that point, God is telling you to go on the inside. If your money hasn't been working for you, it's because you're trying to store it and hold on to it. Remember, God owns everything, you and I own nothing. (This phrase can say, "God owns everything, I *owe* nothing." All you have to do is follow instructions.)

Money cometh wisdom is real; it's everything that enters your heart to sow; it's an assignment! That assignment is to bring us back to life before the curse in the Garden of Eden and to live a debt-free lifestyle where money is not an issue. The same God that brings you up from zero is the God who multiplies what you sow and what's left. God is trying to bring you somewhere, but the question is, are you willing to lay your life down?

10

Submit to the Prophetic Prosperity Anointing

They rose early in the morning, and went forth into the wilder-
ness of Tekoa: and as they went forth, Jehoshaphat stood and
said, Hear me, O Judah, and ye inhabitants of Jerusalem;
Believe in the Lord your God, so shall ye be established;
believe his prophets, so shall ye prosper.

2 Chron. 20:20

Many say they believe in God, but yet, they don't believe

in the one God sent to them with a message. No matter how hard they try to make that work, it doesn't. God won't let you get away with only believing in Him—you have to also believe the prophetic one He sent to you. This is why knowing how to submit to the prophetic prosperity anointing is a major hidden wisdom step of *money cometh.*

God set it up this way for a reason. You cannot bypass Ephesians 4:11-12, which says, "He gave some, apostles; and some, prophets; and some, evangelists; and some, pastors and teachers; (12) For the perfecting of the saints, for the work of the ministry, for the edifying of the body of Christ—" That's the way God designed it. Connection to the five-fold ministry (including apostles, prophets, evangelists, pastors, and teachers) is an important ingredient to your prosperity. Take a look at your life, could it be that you've missed this and didn't believe God's servant? If so, it's time to correct it and align it properly.

When we look at Abram and Lot's relationship in Genesis, we see a great example of what happens when you connect to the prophetic one who God sent. The Lord had given

Abram a word that He would make him a great nation, bless him, make his name great, and make him a blessing (Genesis 12:1-3). If we keep reading to Genesis 13, we see that Lot was with him, and while Abram was rich, Lot, by proximity, also had great possessions.

See Genesis 13:1-6:

And Abram went up out of Egypt, he, and his wife, and all that he had, and Lot with him, into the south. (2) And Abram was very rich in cattle, in silver, and in gold. **[You don't have to guess about this or look for an interpretation. It doesn't say he was rich in spirit. It clearly states that he was rich in cattle, silver, and gold.]**

(3) And he went on his journeys from the south even to Bethel, unto the place where his tent had been at the beginning, between Bethel and Hai; (4) Unto the place of the altar, which he had make there at the first: and there Abram called on the name of the Lord. **[Notice that the things he was rich in didn't take him away from the altar.]**

(5) And Lot also, which went with Abram, had flocks, and

71

herds, and tents. (6) And the land was not able to bear them,
that they might dwell together: for their substance was great, so
that they could not dwell together.

Abram and Lot walked together with lots of possessions, and the town they were in didn't have enough room to hold them both. This proves that when you connect to the prophetic prosperity anointing, the same anointing will come upon *you*. It doesn't matter what financial situation you're in when you start, simply be ready for that leader to establish you through the five-fold ministry gifts.

Another example is in 2 Chronicles 20, where we find Jehoshaphat and his kingdom in danger of a foreign invasion. A prophet, Jahaziel, heard from the Spirit of the Lord and, the morning before the battle, he shared with them this message: "Do not be afraid or discouraged because of this vast army. For the battle is not yours, but God's" (verse 15). The next morning, as they went forth into the wilderness, Jehoshaphat stood and said to the people of Jerusalem, "Believe in the Lord your God, so shall ye be established;

believe his prophets, so shall ye prosper" (verse 20). In other words, he was ensuring them that if they believe in God's promises, they'll be prepared and courageous, and if they believe in His prophet Jahaziel, they'll prosper. They had to believe in *both* God and the one He sent with the message.

In 2 Chronicles 20:25, we see the winning results of Jehoshaphat and the people of Jerusalem hearing and submitting to the prophetic prosperity anointing. It reads: *So Jehoshaphat and his men went to carry off their plunder, and they found among them a great amount of equipment and clothing[d] and also articles of value—more than they could take away. There was so much plunder that it took three days to collect it.*

They had more than enough to collect! This is how God always wanted it to be for his people, especially today, with no limits on their lives.

Follow these hidden wisdom steps that belong to you! Stay holy, give God charge of all your money, don't stop sowing, and submit to the prophetic prosperity anointing at all times.

11

Grow in Prosperity Maturity

Why has the Church not prospered more as a whole? Because ministers, through ignorance, have fought the message of prosperity for years, resulting in an immature Church. They call a certain segment of God's ministers, "prosperity preachers"—and they're right about that part. I'll be a prosperity preacher for the rest of my life. What they don't understand is that God is a prosperity God and Jesus is a prosperity Jesus.

If you still don't believe it, just pick up the Bible and read.

Take a look at the fifth chapter of Luke. The disciples

fished all night long and caught nothing. The prosperity preacher, Jesus, showed up and told them to fish on the other side. When they listened, guess what happened? They gathered more than enough (Luke 5:1-7). That's prosperity! If that doesn't show you the truth, read the sixth chapter of John. When everything looked like it was going wrong, the passage says Jesus already knew what He would do. He looked to the Father, thanked Him, and multiplied what He had in His hands, feeding over five thousand people (John 6:6-11). That's prosperity! Jesus, the ultimate prosperity teacher and manifester, makes known that prosperity is from the Father, and His children have no business being in a bind.

As you grow in prosperity maturity, you'll notice more of it in the Word, and you'll even see that the revelation of *money cometh* is not just about money; it's about the relationship and connection with the Father. From that relationship and connection, God's people receive direction concerning prosperity, freeing them from financial bondage.

Most ministers have not been trained in this area, so they end up fighting against it, causing the Body of Christ to struggle to mature in their personal lives. Too often, ministers don't realize the hypocrisy in speaking against prosperity and then asking to receive an offering from their congregation right after. God's people aren't falling for that! They won't be willing to give as they are led by the Spirit because those types of ministers are not imparting to them how to prosper.

There are three reasons why preachers fight against prosperity:

1. They are religious and don't read for themselves.

2. People are their source, not God.

3. They are jealous.

For these reasons, many of God's people will have to put themselves in a position to bypass the hecklers and those telling them they're wrong and go back to the Bible for themselves.

CONNECT TO A MANIFESTER

While the cultures of this world have come up with their own definitions of what God's prosperity means without biblical backing, the Body of Christ will have to connect to a manifester, one who has been graced for prosperity, in order to grow. (If a leader is not graced for prosperity, he or she will be standing in the way of your prosperity maturity. The word *grace* means to be empowered to do what you couldn't do for yourself.)

When a manifester, who is truly assigned and anointed by God to impart this, teaches on the prosperity of God, three things ought to be removed from your life:

- Distress
- Discontentment
- and Debt (1 Samuel 22:2).

When they are removed, they should be replaced in you with the following:

- Boldness

- Access

- and Confidence (Ephesians 3:12).

Your current condition and how long you've been there does not matter. In your prosperity maturity, it's not only important to submit to the prophetic prosperity anointing but to also stay connected to a manifester and sow. Why? Because a manifester is someone who has already manifested in prosperity and will teach *you* how to do the same.

The ministers who run with me are manifesters. Why? Because they've stayed connected with a genuine manifester anointed by God. Now we know that I am not the source of *money cometh*, Jehovah Jireh is! God is constantly trying to get something to His children, but the worst blockers are ministers who are afraid that sharing this message will knock them off their high horses. But I tell you, it's time's up for those days of holding the Body of Christ back from what is rightfully theirs.

In an earlier chapter, we read about Isaac during the days

of a famine—what did he do? He sowed. That's how you mature in prosperity and get out of your distressed, discontented, and debt condition. You don't get out by praying or praising. You get out by actually connecting to a manifester, maturing as a Christian, and sowing!

Say this out loud, "The days of distress, debt, and discontentment are over in my life. I am walking in boldness, access, and confidence. Money cometh to me now!"

In the next chapter, we'll take your maturity to the next level and dive into a message that has been kept from the Body of Christ for years: apostolic prosperity.

12

Impart Apostolic Prosperity

It is time for the five-fold ministry to have an open discussion of transparency so that the Body of Christ can see what God has designed and aligned.

In Ephesians 4:11-12, Apostle Paul taught: *He gave some, apostles; and some, prophets; and some, evangelists; and some, pastors and teachers; For the perfecting of the saints, for the work of the ministry, for the edifying of the body of Christ.* According to this Word, leaders of the five-fold ministry (apostles, prophets, evangelists, pastors, and teachers) are to mature the Body of Christ so that the work of ministry can be expanded. In Zechariah 1:17, the Lord says, "My cities *through prosperity* shall yet be spread abroad." God uses prosperity to grow the Church and fulfill His Will; however, if a minister does not understand the true aspect and assignment of divine prosperity, he or she will continue to fight against it, and their congregations will never know the truth about what belongs to them.

If we read Isaiah 51:3 as well, we see the outcome He desires: "For the Lord shall comfort Zion: he will comfort all her waste places; and he will make her wilderness like Eden, and her desert like the garden of the Lord; joy and gladness shall be found therein, thanksgiving, and the voice of melody."

If it's true that the Lord shall comfort Zion (the Church) and the cities (His kingdom) shall spread through prosperity—then it also means that His ministers are responsible for imparting and teaching that truth to those following them.

Notice Isaiah 48:17, "Thus saith the Lord, thy Redeemer, the Holy One of Israel; I am the Lord thy God which *teacheth thee to profit*, which leadeth thee by the way that thou shouldest go." This is something that has to be taught. Once it's *taught* by ministers, it can then be caught by the Body of Christ.

What has happened to the Church instead? They have turned to the outside, the world's system, to learn how to prosper, and that shouldn't be—especially when He said His cities would be spread through prosperity. We must not be conformed to this world, but be transformed by the renewing of our minds here so that we can prove or recognize the good, acceptable, and perfect will of God (Romans 12:2).

Apostle Paul made it clear in Ephesians 4:12 that ministers ought to mature the saints to do the work of the ministry so that the Body of Christ can be edified, built, and spread—but none of that is going to happen without prosperity. In other words, we ought to learn about prosperity *in the church*. Going back to Isaiah 48:17, God says, "I am the Lord your God, Who teaches you to profit", so why are believers going outside of the kingdom to learn about their wealth?

Who did Adam and Eve learn prosperity from? God.

Where did the Egyptians learn prosperity from? Prophet Joseph. Pharaoh told Joseph that since God gave him the wisdom of what was going to happen, he was putting him over everything. Pharaoh said that his people would have to go to Joseph just to find out what to do. (Read Genesis 41:39-45.)

Who did the Israelites learn prosperity from when they were in slavery? Moses. He told them the death angel was on the way and to go and borrow what they could. They followed instructions and prospered because of it. (Read Exodus 12:23-36.)

Who did Abraham learn prosperity from? Melchizedek. As soon as Abraham gave the tithes to Melchizedek, the word of the Lord came to him. (Read 14:18-23.)

Who did the disciples learn prosperity from? Jesus. We see it in John 2 when Jesus' mother says to the servants at the wedding "whatever he says to you do it", and with His instructions, the disciples witness the water being turned into wine. We see it in Matthew 14 when He feeds the five thousand with five loaves and two fish. We see it in Matthew 17 when He tells Peter to go fishing and he finds money in the mouth of a fish to pay both of their taxes. (Read John 2:5-10, Matthew 13:15-20, Matthew 14:13-21, and Matthew 17:24-27.)

Who did the early Church of the Book of Acts learn prosperity from? Apostle Peter.

Who did the Church of Christ learn prosperity from? Apostle Paul.

This is how it was designed to be! Sadly, ministers have unconsciously sent their people outside the Church, outside of the kingdom, to the wolves, to learn about prosperity—so instead of training the people, they drain the people. As a result, it has only turned holiness into hustling.

The Church is in this state because the priest continues to reject the knowledge from God that would eventually break their pastoral model of the Church and restructure the Body of Christ back to God's apostolic agenda.

GOD'S APOSTOLIC ORDER

The purpose of an apostle is to structure heaven-to-earth government and open the portal of the supernatural for all those that are connected properly. Under a pastoral model, where pastors are not attached to an apostle, things fall outside of the Will of God. Since the apostle carries the agenda of God, bringing divine order, if a pastor is not attached to an apostle, they are left making up their own agenda. And when you make up the agenda, God is not responsible for funding it. The pastoral model says, "I have to get more people to get more money." The apostolic model says, "I'm going to train who God sends me because God is my source."

When ministers connect to an apostolic agenda, God will begin to open doors and avenues that are beyond what any of us can think. God can get things to us without even needing the money to do it. Until ministers understand this, the people of the Body of Christ will not understand.

Money cometh is an apostolic, prophetic Word from God. It was brought into the earth's realm to bring divine alignment for the leaders of the five-fold ministry. God wants His leaders to prosper so that His people can prosper. There are certain things that must happen in the five-fold ministry *before* it ever happens in the Body of Christ. That's the divine order. How can one impart what they do not have? Jesus couldn't even impart something He didn't have. As soon as He was born, money started looking for Him (Matthew 2:11). Impartation must take place *before* the maturity of the Body of Christ can take place.

Because of improper training, the enemy has emptied the lives of preachers who, although called, cannot fulfill their mission. The support they need has been omitted by not knowing the truth or how to flow with God's ordination of prosperity.

The revelation of *money cometh* is a gift to the Body of Christ. God wants His children in a position where they are rich and have no sorrow or regrets. Ministers should be fighting for what God is doing and putting their egos and old ways of doing things down.

As an apostle, I have laid out a pattern through a jungle. I trusted God. The path has been cleared; the debris has been moved; the ground has been solidified. All you have to do is follow the pattern and forget the ministers who are telling you that you can't do this. Take your seed and combine it with the voice of God. Give God no excuses. We must have boldness (to sow when God says to sow), access (to the peace of God), and confidence (to preach to God's people).

13

Live in Prosperity With No Limits

The hidden wisdom of *money cometh* will advance you in prosperity quickly. Therefore, in preparation for what's to come in your life, I want to invoke instruction and direction on how to live in prosperity with no limits. There are things you'll have to get in place for this to happen.

When you yield to living in prosperity with no limits, it glorifies God, magnifies the Lord Jesus, and satisfies the Holy Ghost. When you are walking in unlimited prosperity, you're a walking testament that God is good and He did not lie.

Headed to a life of God's prosperity, there are four questions you'll have to ask yourself (and answer for yourself) before you arrive:

1. *Am I fully persuaded that prosperity is God's Will for me?*

2. *Am I ready to soak my soul in the fruit of the Spirit?*

3. *Am I willing to wrap my soul in the gifts of the Spirit?*

4. *Am I ready to yield to the prosperity anointing?*

Let's sit with these:

1. Are you fully persuaded that prosperity is God's Will for you?

Abraham was able to receive a prosperity miracle from God because He was fully persuaded that what God promised He was also able to perform (Romans 4:20-22). Abraham knew it was God's Will for his life. From this, we know that if God can get you persuaded about the kind of prosperity He has in store for you then He has no problem getting it to you. God has the ability to make it happen, no matter who comes against you or who says you're not capable of going to that level. When *you* become fully persuaded that God wants you to prosper, it will begin to happen.

[Abraham] staggered not at the promise of God through unbelief; but was strong in faith, giving glory to God; / And being fully persuaded that, what he had promised, he was able also to perform. / And therefore it was imputed to him for righteousness.

Romans 4:20-22

2. Are you ready to soak your soul in the fruit of the Spirit?

One morning, I awakened to the Lord asking: *Are you ready to soak your soul in the fruit of the Spirit?* In other words, He was saying, "Are you ready to soak your soul in love, joy, peace, longsuffering, gentleness, goodness, faith, meekness, and temperance?"

In step one of *money cometh* hidden wisdom, we discussed "holy prosperity". Well, soaking your soul in the fruit of the Spirit is a step in that direction — turning everything over to God. When you do that, you'll be able to handle God's kind of prosperity. Without the fruit of Spirit as your foundation, great prosperity would become a beast in your life, instead of a blessing.

The Father would never give His children anything that would hurt them in the long run. If He learns that you're not ready for it, even though you're a good person who's living right, He won't allow you to step into that level of living in this world. Get into the right position for God to bless you with no limits by meditating on the fruit of the Spirit and making them a part of your everyday thoughts, emotions, imagination, will, and consciousness.

But the fruit of the Spirit is love, joy, peace, longsuffering, gentleness, goodness, faith, / Meekness, temperance: against such there is no law.

Galatians 5:22-23

3. Are you willing to wrap your soul in the gifts of the Spirit?

The same morning I woke to God asking me about soaking my soul in the fruit of the Spirit, He went on to ask, "Are you willing to wrap your soul in the gifts of the Spirit?" In other words, when God brings you into this level of prosperous living, at any moment, you must be able to flow within the spiritual gift of wisdom, word of knowledge, special faith, healing, working of miracles, prophecy, discerning of spirits, divers kinds of tongues, or interpretation of tongues at any given moment. When your soul is wrapped in the gifts of the Spirit, you'll be aligned with the Will of the Lord and be able to make God-led decisions concerning your finances as well.

Now there are diversities of gifts, but the same Spirit. / And
there are differences of administrations, but the same Lord. /
And there are diversities of operations, but it is the same God

which worketh all in all. / But the manifestation of the Spirit is given to every man to profit withal. / For to one is given by the Spirit the word of wisdom; to another the word of knowledge by the same Spirit; / To another faith by the same Spirit; to another the gifts of healing by the same Spirit; / To another the working of miracles; to another prophecy; to another discerning of spirits; to another divers kinds of tongues; to another the interpretation of tongues: / But all these worketh that one and the selfsame Spirit, dividing to every man severally as he will.

1 Corinthians 12:7-11

4. Are you ready to yield to the prosperity anointing?

The last question that morning was, "Are you ready to yield to the prosperity anointing? Now, one thing you must understand about the prosperity anointing is that it's not about *you*. If God is going to deposit large amounts to you, then He must be able to call on you when He needs you. There are particular things you must be willing to do!

It's not all about you doing whatever you want; it's about what He wants. The prosperity anointing is about being ready to be led by the Holy Spirit with instructions on what to do with the prosperity you were given.

***

I've asked and answered each of these questions for myself and it has yielded much success. I can tell you now that if you've been paying attention to what you've been reading here and you're willing to take action toward each step and lesson, then you'll receive every answer you need concerning your dilemmas and hold-ups. I speak from revelation and experience — with this truth and willingness under your belt, you are ready to live in prosperity with no limits.

DR. LEROY THOMPSON SR.

PART II

Extended Words of Wisdom

6 Principles of Prosperity

1. MOVE BEYOND NATURAL KNOWLEDGE.

Everything in life is based on knowledge. However, most times we are dealing with secular knowledge instead of supernatural knowledge—which is the knowledge that comes from God.

Second Peter 1:3-4 says, "According as his divine power hath given unto us all things that pertain unto life and godliness, through the *knowledge of him* that hath called us to glory and virtue: Whereby are given unto us exceeding great and precious promises: that by these ye might be partakers of the divine nature, having escaped the corruption that is in the world through lust." Knowledge is important, but it's God's kind of knowledge that matters most.

For knowledge of Him to be beneficial, it must be meditated upon. Meditation is how you eat the Word. In other words, you can't digest that knowledge if you don't spend time meditating on it and hearing His voice. And you cannot walk by faith until you hear properly.

Meditation will cause you to flow into John 6:63: "It is the spirit that quickeneth; the flesh profiteth nothing: the words that I speak unto you, they are spirit, and they are life." Hearing the voice of the Son of God is your first source of faith. His words are spirit and life. With that comes revelation, and we can only live from that revealed knowledge from the Holy Ghost.

Information, meditation, and revelation are all parts of your preparation. From there, you'll move from impartation to manifestation to demonstration and application. Then, there's a graduation, and you'll find yourself in the midst of a financial visitation. And that financial visitation will bring you into a process called glorification!

2. MONEY COMETH IS AN ABSOLUTE.

Money comes because that's what money does—it's an absolute. It's a declaration of what is. If we believe this to be true, then what are we, the Body of Christ, doing? Have we forfeited our purposes for money? I believe God wants His children to use their gifts to take over territories in the world's system, and while we will need money to do so, the enemy has misled many into believing that they must first use their gifts to go get the money. But the truth is, *money cometh* because that's what money does!

All you're supposed to do is what you were sent to do.

In what image were you created? God's image, according to Genesis 1:27. What does God need? He needs nothing.

So, why are believers in desperate need of anything? You have no needs if God has no needs. Allow that to sink in. "My God shall supply all your need according to his riches in glory by Christ Jesus," reads Philippians 4:19.

Reach →

The average believer has boarded up their windows of heaven with their own prayers because most of their prayers are based on what they *think* they need rather than aligned with God's Will.

The revelation of *money cometh* puts us back in the Garden of Eden, before the curse, where praying for our needs didn't exist because everything was provided.

Money cometh is not a prayer or a plan, it's a demand and an absolute. The plan is already fulfilled.

---

3. WE ARE ALREADY WHERE WE ARE GOING.

The apostolic and prophetic *money cometh* move we are in is a "kingdom culture". In this culture, you have to be willing to challenge your current status in order to change.

There are four things we must be willing to do:

1. not be afraid to trust in God

2. show a willingness to cross thresholds

3. look to cross lines that have been drawn

4. lose what feels safe and comfortable

We are on a journey, but we are also already where we are going. We simply need to understand it and act like it, recognizing that God has already established his position concerning our prosperity.

4. MY SOUL KNOWETH RIGHT WELL.

In Psalm 139:14, the psalmist David exalts the power of God, praying, "I will praise thee; for I am fearfully and wonderfully made: marvellous are thy works; and that my soul knoweth right well."

Someone who understands how fearfully and wonderfully made they are, as well as how marvelous God's works are, embodies a prosperous life. David was fully convinced that God had made him fearfully and wonderfully and that God's works are marvelous, so he wrote, "My soul knows right (or very) well." Similarly, your soul must be fully convinced of God's divine prosperity. You must know in your meditation, mindset, imagination, consciousness, and will that prosperity in your body and life is real and right, and that it pleases God without a doubt.

5. LORD, BRING MY SOUL OUT OF PRISON.

In Psalm 143:7, we see David saying to God, "Bring my soul out of prison, that I may praise thy name: the righteous shall compass me about; for thou shalt deal bountifully with me."

If you're not prospering as you should, your soul is in prison. Therefore, get your thinking, speaking, will, emotions, and imagination out of this prison. Prosperity is a soul benefit. Satan has been holding prosperity back through your soul. "For the enemy hath persecuted my soul," writes David in Psalm 143:3-4, "he hath smitten my life down to the ground; he hath made me to dwell in darkness, as those that have been long dead. Therefore is my spirit overwhelmed within me; my heart within me is desolate."

In order to see your prosperity, you must first stop the enemy from persecuting your soul. In other words, your spirit has it, but it can't bring it to you until your soul is free of this prison. What God has for you can't get through your soul because your thinking and confessing are wrong. You use the words *can't* and *not able* too much. When your soul is out of order, you shut your spirit down.

Say it aloud, "Lord, bring my soul out of prison!"

6. SOWING IS GOD SHOWING HIMSELF IN US.

Your life is more valuable than the lifestyle you're trying to chase. If God can put breath in your lungs, you should be sure He can put money in your pocket. The money is easy. Jesus says, "Take no thought for your life, what ye shall eat, or what ye shall drink; nor yet for your body, what ye shall put on. Is not the life more than meat, and the body than raiment?" (Matthew 6:25). Your life is much more valuable than the things you're looking for in this world.

"Behold the fowls of the air: for they sow not, neither do they reap, nor gather into barns; yet your heavenly Father feedeth them. Are ye not much better than they?" Jesus asks in Matthew 6:26. You are better than the birds of the air. They neither sow nor reap; they don't get to do as God does, but yet God is taking care of them. What is He saying to us here? "Sowing is Me showing Myself in you." When we sow, we get a chance to be like Him.

In 2 Corinthians 9:7, we read, "Every man according as he purposeth in his heart, so let him give; not grudgingly, or of necessity: for God loveth a cheerful giver." This means our seed is not for our needs, because God's got that. Every time we sow, God reveals His nature and shows us how to walk in His nature. Ultimately, he desires to put us in the plan above the plans of our own.

30 Decrees of Hidden Wisdom

I declare that...

1. *God is my source, my supply, my way in and my way out, my reasoning, and my solution.*

2. *Money will never have authority over me or tell me what I can or can't do. I will have authority over money, just like Jesus. I will walk by faith when it comes to my finances.*

3. *Profound manifestations and demonstrations are on the horizon for me now!*

4. *I'm out of debt, out of distress, and out of discontentment.*

5. *I have boldness, access, and confidence.*

6. *God is wrapping me in money wisdom. He is giving me discernment on which money moves to make.*

7. *I'll have as much fun giving as I'll have receiving.*

8. *The prosperity anointing is upon me. I am anointed to prosper. Prosperity is God's divine will for me as His child, and I have a right to have this in my mind and imagination.*

9. *I come to grips with the truth that it's not wrong to want the God kind of prosperity that belongs to me.*

10. *Whatever has been a struggle will now become easier. No struggle will reign over me anymore.*

11. *From this day forward, the Lord will make everything in my hands prosper (Gen. 39:1-3). God is putting a prosperity touch on me, and whatever I touch will prosper.*

12. *My prosperity is holy, and because of that, it will never stop coming to me.*

13. *The Holy Spirit is in charge of all my finances.*

14. *I will remember God in every transaction.*

15. *From this day forward, my life will be different. God is about to take money out of the wrong living hands and put it in the hands of His children.*

16. *I'll never be broke another day in my life.*

17. *My life is centered on the fact that God owns everything. I own nothing! The earth is the Lord's, and the fullness thereof; the world, and they that dwell therein.*

18. *Money cometh in my life because that's what money does.*

19. *The windows of heaven are opened over me because I am constantly aligning with the Will of God.*

20. *I have prosperity maturity. Prosperity maturity cometh to me now!*

21. *All financial crises must leave my life now!*

22. *I am already where I am going.*

23 *My hour of financial freedom has come! I'm free, and prosperity belongs to me. It is already mine.*

24. God will use me financially.

25. My soul is out of prison and I am prospering as I should.

26. There are no more holes in my bag!

27. The famines are over for me. God is depositing something in me, and I'm going to know it's over like I've never known before.

28. The Word of God is performing surgery on me in any place that isn't prospering. God is putting me in a position where I can walk in the real prosperity He has for me.

29. I believe what God is saying; I believe what God is doing; I believe what God promised, and my actions are backing up what I am saying. It's releasing God's heavenly covenant in my life.

30. I am being released and escorted into the next glory dimension of prosperity. There is nothing too big, too hard, or too fast for God.

A Prophetic Word for Now

It's time to move into another realm. It's time to move into different revelations so that I can put you in a place of the remnant.

There are people who love Me that are supposed to stand out above the crowd. Right now, I'm putting My hand on you. I'm putting My mind in you. And I'm clearing your steps to walk higher.

So get ready for explosive manifestation in your life. I'm your God, and you're My people, and I believe you're ready to go.

Today, I speak to you by revelation knowledge. I speak to you in an apostolic anointing that you'll be flowing through from this day forward. You'll be changing and shifting, lifting and moving in higher dimensions of My Spirit.

I've been looking for you. I've been looking for people who are ready to go and who are ready to flow, people who are ready to grow in the dimension of My Spirit—so that My anointing may move you in a deeper understanding of who you are.

– God, Our Father

About the Author

Louisiana native, Dr. (Apostle) Leroy Thompson Sr. is the Pastor of Word of Life Christian Center and Chief overseer of Leroy Thompson Ministerial Association (LTMA) and Ever Increasing Word Ministries.

With a strong calling from God, Apostle Thompson travels the world taking the message of financial freedom to the Body of Christ by holding Money Cometh to You Conferences. He truly believes that God's financial abundance is for every believer. He is the author of several books, including his bestseller "Money Cometh! To The Body of Christ."

Apostle Thompson not only believes but also knows from experience that the key to a successful ministry is the combination of praying in the spirit, living and teaching the Word of Faith, and following after the leadership of the Holy Ghost.

He has been happily married to his lovely wife, Mrs. Carolyn A. Thompson, for over 50 years. They have four children — Leroy Jr. (Shantel), Shauna (Jesse), Donavan (Nakia), and Darnell (Deirdre) — who serve full-time in the ministry along with their parents.

Other Books by Dr. Leroy Thompson, Sr.

Money Cometh! To The Body of Christ

Sow & Grow Rich

Never Go After Money

Framing Your World with the Word of God

No More Empty Hands

You're Not Broke You Have A Seed Money Thou Art Loosed!

How to Find Your Wealthy Place

I'll Never Be Broke Another Day in My Life

Money With A Mission

What To Do When Your Faith Is Challenged

The Voice of Jesus—Speaking God's Word With Authority
Framing Your World With the Word of God

Order these books and other products by Dr. Leroy Thompson online at www.eiwm.org.

If this book has been a blessing to you or if you would like to see more of the Ever Increasing Word Ministries product line, please visit us on our website at www.eiwm.org.

Become a Partner

WHAT DOES IT MEAN TO BECOME A PARTNER?

YOU ARE IN AGREEMENT WITH THIS VISION AND THIS VISION IS IN AGREEMENT WITH YOU!

Where there is no vision, the people perish: but he that keepeth

the law, happy is he.

Proverbs 29:18

PARTNERSHIP PRIVILEGES

- Regular prayer from this ministry for your success and victory

- Monthly impartation and update letter from us

- Monthly CD or MP3 teaching from Apostle Thompson

- An official FINANCIAL FREEDOM Membership Card that enables you to a 20% discount on any products ordered from this ministry

- Leroy Thompson TV Financial Freedom Partnership Portal: Gaining access to videos and messages from Apostle Leroy Thompson, designated for the partners

- Most importantly, you will be exercising the impartation and information you receive to produce a God-fulfilled life!

To become a partner, visit www.eiwm.org/partnership, today.

CPSIA information can be obtained
at www.ICGtesting.com
Printed in the USA
JSHW071150200623
43445JS00003B/4

9 781931 804011